Harrow:
London Poems of Convalescence

A Collection of Poems
by Tijan M. Sallah

Global Hands Publishing 2014

Harrow: London Poems of Convalescence is published by:
Global Hands Publishing
Room 24A
Innovation Centre
Leicester, LE1 5XY

Tel: 01162577952
Email: publishing@global-hands.co.uk
Web: www.global-hands.co.uk

Typeset by: Global Hands Publishing
Cover Design by: Daniel Sturrock

A catalogue for this book is available from the British Library.

ISBN 978-0-9574073-4-3

Other Books by Tijan M. Sallah

Poetry Collections
When Africa Was a Young Woman (1980, Writers Workshop, India)
Kora Land (1989, Three Continents Press, USA)
Dreams of Dusty Roads (1993, Three Continents Press, USA)
Dream Kingdom: New and Selected Poems (2007, Africa World Press, USA)

Short Stories
Before the New Earth (1988, Writers Workshop, India)

Biography
Chinua Achebe: Teacher of Light (2003, Africa World Press, USA)

Ethnography
Wolof: The Heritage Library of African Peoples (1996, Rosen Publishing, USA)

Poetry Anthologies (Edited)
New Poets of West Africa (1995, Malthouse Press, Nigeria)
The New African Poetry (co-edited with Tanure Ojaide) (1999, Lynne Rienner Publishers, USA)

In memory of
Chinua Achebe and Nadine Gordimer,
two dear friends; two great African heroes.

About the Author

Tijan M. Sallah is the Gambia's most famous living poet and one of Africa's most significant writers. His works have appeared in several major African poetry and short story anthologies. Professor Wumi Raji of Nigeria's Obafemi Awolowo University recently edited a book of critical perspectives on his writings published by Cambria Press titled, "Tijan M. Sallah and Literary Works from the Gambia." Sallah is a Ph.D- trained economist and works for the World Bank.

Table of Contents

FOREWORD 8

HERE I LIE NOW 12

THE NIGHTS CAN BE LONG 14

TRIBUTE TO THE BODY-CARPENTER 16

MY NIECE SAYS 18

THE NURSE SAYS 19

NEXT TO GOD, THE DOCTOR 20

GOD SAVE US 22

I MUST NOT LOOK DOWN 24

SOME FRIENDS SAY 29

I LIE DOWN 31

MAD COW 33

NEAR-DEATH EXPERIENCE 35

THE AFRICAN PENGUINS 36

THE MAID THAT BRINGS 38

ENLIGHTENMENT 39

A LESSON OF HISTORY 41

UNABLE TO STAND 44

WHEN SHALL I SEE THE SUN? 45

FOREWORD

Harrow – the child of a harrowing experience in London. On October 12, 2000, while transiting overnight in London, I stepped out of the Sheraton Heathrow Hotel to get a quick dinner. As a pedestrian, I felt the rain drizzle slowly, and visibility was hazy. While crossing the road to the Fina Gas Station, I got absorbed in unawares. Within the twitch of an eye, I suddenly found myself hit with fearsome force by a speeding saloon car. I was thrown in the air and violently landed on the tarmac. I thought I had met my fate. I sustained extensive fractures on my left femur, and bruises and lacerations. I was lucky.

Fortuitously, the driver stopped, and called for

help. An ambulance showed up one hour later—and rushed me on a stretcher to the West Middlesex University Hospital in Hounslow, London. There, I underwent surgery; then got transferred to The Clementine Churchill Hospital in Sudbury Hill, Harrow, for recovery.

My wife was shocked. My two little kids (then only 6 and 2 years old), faced with the experience of my long absence, knew something unusual had happened. My nieces domiciled in London, Jainaba and Dr. Fatou Mama Manneh, and my British friends, Christopher and Isabelle Ward of Devon, kept my spirits high throughout this trying episode. My ultra-shocked, then 86 year old, sage-father, consumed by worry, telephoned saying he prayed for a quick mend.

I was amazed and humbled by the many telephone calls of support from several prominent friends and colleagues. The world famous novelist, the late Chinua Achebe—it was his 70th birthday celebration at Bard College in upstate New York – to which I was invited--- called to wish me quick recovery. Achebe himself, few years earlier, survived a debilitating car accident, which confined him to a wheel chair. On return to the US, I nursed my wounds for over eight months, and followed a daily regime of pain-killers and physical therapy to learn to walk again. I was uplifted. People are good.

The poems in this volume were inspired by that tragic episode. They have never been published in a single volume. They were written in Harrow while convalescing from the accident. Every day, I wrote one poem and read it when the Ward family came. It became a liberating ritual, a catharsis. I wrote the poems in rhymes with the utmost simplicity, quite unusual from my regular free verse. I believe many readers will find comfort in their lonely vision—as idioms of hope-- *as poems of looking up when you are down.*

Sudbury Hill, Harrow, United Kingdom
October 31, 2000

Potomac, Maryland, USA
August 20, 2014

HERE I LIE NOW

Here I lie now in Harrow,
Licking over my sorrows,
Like a dog whose injured dignity
Makes him howl silently in pity.

Life has a way of coming to a bump,
When I am speeding aimlessly on the hump
Of the quest for coins and fame.
For why should I be suddenly lame?

Here I lie now in Harrow;
I might just as well have been in a wheelbarrow.
For time ticks slowly to the aching
Of joints and muscles, and the body slowly
waking.

My friends, the Wards, bring books and shoes.

Their love takes away my mind from the blues.
They joke about the Dickensian hell I have been in;
I look up and see warmth in their faces full to the brim.

THE NIGHTS CAN BE LONG

The nights can be long when in pain,
And the temperature and bedding never right.
And comfort can only be a pact in vain,
And sweat and helpless turns to feel alright.

And I feel tonight like a throbbing newborn,
But with a history; so without the garment of
innocence.
I am conscious of the past, but helplessly forlorn;
Waiting for time to unfold to morning in patience.

The nights can be long when in pain,
And wakefulness can be a feverish nightmare of
waiting.
And anxiousness can be a religion of the heart in
vain.

But why should my pain and time be mating?

The nights can be long when in pain.
The nurse interrupts; thoughts shift to tablets.
For a while, at least, the heart throbs, and one is sane.
And I remember the addiction to pills and the water goblet.

TRIBUTE TO THE BODY-CARPENTER

So I pay my tribute to the body-carpenter.
After my mortal furniture is broken,
I need his nails and hammer.
I need his bandages as token.

So I sing praises to the body-carpenter,
For he has x-rayed my body-furniture,
Taken blood samples; stabilized my leg.
Now I wait for his genius to rebuild me at the peg.

My body is no better than broken furniture.
Wobbly it is, and its music squeaks.
Looking like some animated painful picture,
I move slowly making sure nothing breaks.

I know I will be left with scars;

But who knows a carpenter who does not leave
marks?
I pay my tribute to the carpenter of scars,
Who joins muscles and bones with herbs and bark.

MY NIECE SAYS

My niece says it is just a fracture.
She is a nurse, dealing with ailments of heart and lung.
No wonder she diagnoses that my present strictures
Are milder than her usual medical dance and song.

She is so used to dealing with near-death cases,
That a fracture is slightly off the severity base.
Bones and tissues will heal; normality will return.
Death is not waiting to be born.

I know mine is just a fracture,
But not all fractures are just fractures.
Thank God for sparing my skull and spine,
Else I would not have been supine.

THE NURSE SAYS

The nurse says, because I walk funny,
I must have stayed at the pub long last night.
But as far as I know I have not been jolly,
Having been lying in an orthopedic ward the past seven nights.

The nurse must have a sense of humor,
To confuse a patient's walk
With that of a teetotaler recovering from stupor.
Besides, I am so coherent in my talk.

I do not know what to say to the nurse,
For life can be sometimes playing horse.
All I know is the nurse jokes with a certain passion;
I can only think of it as compassion.

NEXT TO GOD, THE DOCTOR

When in pain, next to God, is the doctor.
The universe collapses when pain soars in the nerves and bones,
And all one could do is to summon the nurse as the proctor.
The doctor's words ring like God's trombones,
Every syllable must be weighed with an ounce of good measure.
And the prescriptions must be held with the sacredness of treasure.

When in pain, next to God, is the doctor.
And one is reminded of Epicurus's dictum:
That Nature bestowed on humanity
Two sovereign principles – pain and pleasure.

It is in our nature to seek money, fame, wine and
good posture,
And to avoid snakes, scorpions and pinches on the
rectum.

GOD SAVE US

God, save us from the fiery temper of this
windward gale,
That roared all night like a hungry lion, scaring us
from sleep,
That rumbled in garbage cans across my window
sill,
That fractured tree limbs to block roads and rails.

God, save me, for fear made me call the nurse,
When the thunder outside drowned my body
pains.
And all I did was, from deep sleep, to pause,
And wait for the gruesome showers to gently wane.

God, save Britain from the bad temper of this
windward gale,

For swaths of the South are in flood alert.
Nature's revenge dogged Kent, Sussex, Wales, and other parts.
Why should global warming violently so ship-sail?

God, save humanity from mindless terror on nature,
Else, we are doomed to suffer its revenge and torture.

I MUST NOT LOOK DOWN
(Collingbrook Bypass, Middlesex)

I must not look down at the trash now,
For that night I felt like dignified trash.

I lay by the roadside semi-conscious somehow,
Waiting for the ambulance to come to the site of
crash.

The driver was maniacally speeding in a cold,
damp night.
And I the lone pedestrian was heading to my
temporary abode.
The light at the Fina Gas station was carnival
bright,
And all I remember was gruesome violence come
on me in full load.

For a moment, I thought, as I flew in the air,
That death has suddenly beckoned me to final rest.
But, thank Great Kindness, I was half-spared.
I now have to reflect and anticipate the best.

The driver stopped to cover me with his jacket.
Sour hospitality, at least, he was not a hit-and-run.
Conscience can sometimes police evil with a
bracket.
I lay there, stunned, delirious with pain-rum.

The police came and covered me with hotel-
borrowed blankets.
They called the ambulance which was an hour late.
They interrogated the driver and issued a ticket.
I lay there unsure of what will befall my fate.

The ambulance came and rescued me from
hypothermia.
I was belted on a stretcher, but in hellish pain.

At the West Middlesex University Hospital, after
miles of macadamia,
They x-rayed my leg and chest; pinched for blood
with a pin.

They diagnosed that I had circular fractures on my
thigh,
And will need to stabilize my leg before surgery.
Of course, I could greet this only with a sigh,
Knowing much remained to mend through
drudgery.

Wheeled to an open ward of ten patients,
Where old men lay waiting, contemplating of
death,
And young men dreamed of pubs and pants,
I joined their shared drama of agony, breath to
breath.

An old man howled in infectious pain.

His agony spread; his cry ringing in vain.
"Help," he cried, in shivering voice;
Then moaned, staring listlessly, and then in poise.

Another was attached to shots of morphine.
Pain killers had their field day in this restless ward.
I said to myself, why can pain be so inanely supreme,
To drown patients in sobbing, with eerie lost of words.

And so there I lay like a wounded animal,
Awaiting surgery in painful delirium.
Afraid of the move, sedentary but not numb,
I hope for Great Kindness to rescue me from pandemonium.

One of the doctors said, on Sunday, it will be done.
The surgery team was assembled.

On Sunday, the team met and stitched me to the
bone.
I woke from general anesthesia, half-sleep, but in a
tremble.

I rose from sleep, amused, at their white uniforms.
Half dazed; half in grace, and ready for the reform.

SOME FRIENDS SAY

Some friends say I should sue the driver,
But I do not want to create a paradise for lawyers
I do not want to be in their garrulous game.
I do not want to trundle to the courts for fame.

Some friends say I must be a fool to ignore my pa
and suffering,
To pilfer my agony in silent sobbing.
But should muscles and bones be ever for sale?
Or else why should we not offer the human for
retail?

Some friends say I should sue the driver,
Pilfer his pocket for pushing me close to being
cadaver.
Make his wallet feel the price of unsafety;

Make him sit every evening and read the rules of road safety.

I LIE DOWN

I lie down
I must not frown.
I am hospital bound.
I must heal, and be sound.

The will is hobbled
By poverty of means.
I lie in this bubble,
Etherized to be weaned.

I lie down.
I must not frown.
The doctor arrives in a white gown.
Who knows a better healer in town?

Then gently, gently, call them in.
For I am growing thin.

And pain surges from within.

And pain tries to do me in.

MAD COW

My British friend jokingly said,
While I was in my sick-bed,
He is unsure why the French make so much noise
about mad cow,
When they are already all mad anyhow.

The French boycott British beef,
When the science says it is safe.
Even as the British public has returned to old
habits,
Of pleasing the palate with steak and other meaty
bits.

Lord Phillips' report on TV raised the issue.
My friend could not but pursue
The fine line between free speech, science and
panicky reactions,

When there is a public scare and similar actions.

Lord Phillips' BSE Report argued there was cover
up,
In Tory's long denial of CJD and BSE.
To placate profit and trade, they bungled it up,
While information-deprived victims died of the
disease.

I said to myself, perhaps the French are after all not
wrong,
To play it safe, until the science is strong.

NEAR-DEATH EXPERIENCE

Near-death experience can be religious;
It turned my eyes to the obvious.
That the creator on high
Loves us to be nigh.
That mindless seeking of silver and fortune
Can lead to spiritual misfortune.

It seems moderating the passions is the key,
When we are soaked in world-lust, engulfed in the tempting sea.
We should pray daily and be mindful,
If nothing, to our own soul-yearnings, be careful.

THE AFRICAN PENGUINS

While nursing my fractures on my wooden chair,
I turned on to Sky News with its recurrent fair.
The reporter spoke of the African penguins at the Bristol zoo.
Black-feathered, white-breasted birds walking like humans in legs of two.

The scientists put electronic eggs in their nests;
They collect information on their incubation habits through their tests.
Signals are sent, then relayed by cable to a computer.
I said, dumb birds, tricked by similarity, warm as butter.

It seems a strange bedmate, these cryptic eggs
under their buttocks
That does espionage to satisfy human curiosity
Through gadgets, wires, and other transmitting
blocks.
Poor penguins, tricked by technology warm with
familiarity.

THE MAID THAT BRINGS

The maid that brings me the hospital meal
Tells me she is an Indian Tamil,
And that nearby, over the hill;
Was the Harrow School,
Where children of the British elite
Get groomed for the high seat.

She said many Asian children are there,
Dressed in garbs, children of empire,
Tutored in philosophy and bourgeois etiquette,
The new rainbow-Britain drawn from the global
sphere.

I said to myself, Britain is really a great place,
Open to all the world's cultures and races,
Welded by this English, this maxim-tongue,
That flows like water, and to all belongs.

ENLIGHTENMENT

Today, the sun is out and bright,
And it feels like the Enlightenment.
London, commerce-city, is a shining light,
Memory-loaded from a long cerebrality and
thought-internment.

I could see John Locke and his Treatise,
And other men in periwigs with thought expertise,
Wrestling with the future, especially the
foundations of law and order,
Including the liberty jewels, the sacred pillar of the
polis.

I could see heretics questioning *doxas,*
Those handed-down tablets, like the logs of Moses.
I could see them cast sunlight at all the boxes,
To ensure truth is open in all places.

Today, the sun is out and bright.
The chattering castes are out until midnight,
Arguing over ideas, belief, and the new,
Thought and counter-thought, mixed into a rational stew.

A LESSON OF HISTORY

I think of multitudinous wild fruits ripening in
Summer;
I am reminded of the perils and victorious world of
the English explorer.
I am reminded of vanquished, colorful worlds,
forged by syllables, under the scepter.
Of resisting hordes, breaking from their fetters.

I think of all the tribes that merged on the isles.
Angles, Vikings, Normans, Celts, Roman, in miles.
I am reminded of the folly of those that clamor
purity.
The isles are a complex babble of hybridity.

Even in this hospital ward.

The assimilated and unassimilated mix in rich reward.
English accents flutter with pepper and salt,
Into a patois, rich and satisfying as malt.

And there are the latecomers.
They bring curry and rumba to initial skeptical corners.
Soon they became king. England invaded by the magic
Of aboriginal histories, a rich panache of lore, craft, and lyric.

I am reminded of the isles
As a refurbished playground for the beauty of Empire.
No debate. Empires also smell of aboriginal skeletons. Open the archives, files…
Look through only, so long as you can bear the stones and fire.

I lie down here in this land of Empire.
After it has retreated, reflected, retired.
I am reminded of Hindustan and Bantustans,
Of English incursions into indigenous lands.

I am reminded of suppressed histories, buried tongues.
Even of the Irish; lost indigenous songs.
England will become the world it vanquished.
Convergence is the future of the invader and the anguished.

UNABLE TO STAND

Unable to stand on my feet,
I swallowed the throes of defeat.
The urine bottle comes to my bed,
And also, the jelly and food I was fed.
Shots of morphine daily, they said,
To postpone the pain, and then the maid.

Dependency is the child of paralysis;
I have to come this after much analysis.
Like a child, one relearns routine.
And pride must sleep in the body's palanquin.
One must look at the willow
Outside the broad window,
How it looks up slowly, slowly
After aggressed by the snow,
Until it recovers strength boldly,
And returns to past beauty in a bow.

WHEN SHALL I SEE THE SUN?

When shall I see the sun again?
When shall I see the sun?
Autumnal leaves break into a rainbow train.
When shall I see the sun?

North London is blustery cold;
Even the feathery pigeons lust for the sun.
I must look out and appear bold,
For sunlight is rare here as a unicorn.

When shall I see the sun?
The clouds parade in white, blue and gray.
A lonely crow shuttles in search of sun.
Must I, like the crow, just obey?

When shall I see the sun?
Town-folks huddle in dark woolen jackets.

Pigeons cluster warmly in the sky in fun.
Should I presume they head to market?

When shall I see the sun again?
When shall I see the sun?
Autumnal leaves break in a carnival train.
When shall I see the sun?

Other books published by Global Hands Publishing

Innocent Questions is a collection of poems from Dr. Momodou Sallah, a Gambian senior lecturer in Youth and Community Development at De Montfort University in Leicester, UK. It deals with issues ranging from the dreams of an African school boy to the frustrations of a consummate professional in Babylon. The poems give voice to a continent, the frustrations, the anger, the realities and the struggle for hope.

The Graveyard Cannot Pray is an autobiographical account by Dr. Baba Galleh Jallow, who is currently Assistant Professor of African History at Creighton University, Omaha, Nebraska, USA. The book deals with one man's battle to save his daughter from Female Circumcision. Perhaps the first to articulate the battle against FGM from an African male perspective, *The Graveyard Cannot Pray* throws into sharp relief the conflict between older and younger generation of Africans; communal conflict and its resolution among the Futa Fulani; the Fulani notion of son-hood, and the potential complications between the sanctity of tradition versus that of faith. Dr. Isatou Touray, Executive Director of the Gambia Committee on Traditional Practices Affecting the Health of Women and Children (GAMCOTRAP) wrote the preface for this book.

A Harvest of Gambian Lines: A poetry Anthology, edited by Abdoulie Jatta and Musa Jallow with a preface by Tijan M. Sallah, is a vibrant new anthology of poems by young Gambians. It is a must read for anyone interested in the growth of creativity in West Africa's tiny country.

Lightning Source UK Ltd.
Milton Keynes UK
UKOW04f1010141114

241602UK00002B/34/P

9 780957 407343

www.ingramcontent.com/pod-product-compliance
Ingram Content Group UK Ltd.
Pitfield, Milton Keynes, MK11 3LW, UK
UKHW042009190726
13854UKWH00005B/2226